Celiac Cookbook

Enjoy recipes that don't contain gluten

BY

Julia Chiles

License Notes

Table of Contents

Introduction

It has been proven that gluten can be very detrimental to one's health. What many people do not know is that several foods contain gluten. That is why it is essential to be aware of the foods that contain gluten and what you should eat instead of these foods.

If you are looking for some delicious gluten-free recipes, then you have stumbled upon the right place. When eating gluten-free, you must eat food that tastes great while still being nutritious. You can do this by using the recipes in this cookbook. These recipes are some of the best recipes that you will ever find for cooking delicious gluten-free meals.

You can enjoy these recipes with your family and friends, knowing that they do not contain gluten while still tasty.

This cookbook is full of some of these delicious gluten-free recipes. If you want to learn how to make incredible meals, then this book is the one for you.

After your first time trying one of these recipes, you will never be able to resist them again. When trying some of the recipes in this book, you probably will not even realize that they are gluten-free. It is challenging to tell that some of these foods use flour or other wheat products. These recipes taste just like the wheat-based version, so it is hard for people to determine what they are missing.

Gluten is very detrimental to one's health, so it is important to only eat the foods that are good for you. When you are looking for some delicious meals that do not contain gluten, then you can use these recipes. These recipes will allow you to cook some of the best meals that you have ever tasted.

The recipes in this cookbook are some of the best that you will ever find on the Internet. These recipes are so easy to follow, so even if you have never cooked before, you will be able to prepare them.

Celiac recipes are a great way to get people to try healthier foods. The reality is that many people do not want to eat healthy meals because they do not taste good. When you use some of the recipes in this cookbook, you will change that mindset. These recipes taste delicious and are very healthy at the same time.

If you are looking for a way to make healthy meals, then this is the book for you. You can make some of these meals for your family or even for yourself on a regular basis.

These recipes will allow you to enjoy some of the best meals that you have ever had. These dishes will be tasty, and you will love the way that they taste. You will be able to enjoy your food on a daily basis!

Breakfast Recipes

The breakfasts provide the best options for starting the day healthier. Some also offer the most accessible means of saving time in the kitchen yet enjoying meals crucial for health as starters. Most of the ingredients are easily accessible.

Scrambled Avocado Eggs with Salmon

Starting a great morning requires easy-to-prepare dishes and, therefore, essential to consider the Scrambled Avocado Eggs with Salmon as an option. The meal boasts energy ingredients that will keep you stable, solid, and active all day long.

Servings: 2

Preparation time: 15 minutes

Ingredients:

- 100 g smoked and diced salmon
- ¼ tsp. pepper
- ½ cored avocado
- 4 eggs
- 1 tsp. coconut oil
- 2 tbsp. chopped chives
- ¼ tsp. salt

Directions:

Core the avocado and dice half of the pulp. Whisk the eggs together.

Mix the salmon with the eggs.

Heat the coconut oil in a sizable pan and fry the scrambled eggs in it.

Garnish with avocado and chives.

Season with salt and pepper and serve.

Hearty Breakfast Casserole

Hearty meals and crowd-pleasers are all you desire every fine morning. In these breakfast casseroles, you will not miss the hearty touched incorporated within them through a proper set of combined nutritious ingredients. You can also consider making the meal ahead and therefore save your morning time for other crucial duties.

Servings: 12

Preparation time: 40 minutes

Ingredients:

- ¼ tsp. hot paprika powder
- 12 eggs
- ¼ tsp. salt
- 1 onion, chopped
- 1 diced sweet potato
- 100 g chopped spinach
- 3 peeled and chopped shallots
- ¼ tsp. pepper

Directions:

Preheat the oven to 355°F.

Beat the eggs and whisk them together. Then season the egg mixture with paprika powder, salt, and pepper.

Grease a baking pan. Place the spinach, shallots, onion, and sweet potato in the baking pan.

Pour the egg mixture over the sizable pan and bake the casserole for 35 minutes.

Chia Pudding with Cocoa

Every breakfast should come with a robust dish loaded with nutritious and healthy ingredients. Chia pudding with cocoa incorporates a properly combined set of elements, including coconut milk, chia seeds, honey, among other crucial aspects. They are a more significant source of incorporating sweetness into the entire dish.

Servings: 2

Preparation time: 10 minutes + 60 minutes refrigeration time

Ingredients:

- 1 tsp. vanilla powder
- 2 cups coconut milk
- 6 tbsp. chia seeds
- 2 tsp. cocoa powder
- 1 tbsp. honey
- ½ tsp. cinnamon
- A handful of fresh berries (optional)

Directions:

Mix and stir all ingredients.

Put the pudding in the refrigerator for 60 minutes.

If you like, you can garnish the pudding with fresh berries.

Vegetable Buffer

Vegetable buffer is a combination of the most delicious ingredients, and the final taste is filling. The meal is crucial for the entire family and will ensure a healthier lifestyle, especially for the kids.

Servings: 4

Preparation time: 20 minutes

Ingredients:

- ½ tsp. cinnamon
- 2 tsp. salt
- ¼ cup coconut flour
- 1 tbsp. ghee
- 5 zucchinis
- 1 tsp. pepper
- 1 egg, beaten
- ¼ tsp. cayenne pepper

Directions:

Grate the zucchinis and let rest for 10 minutes. Then squeeze out and mix with the remaining ingredients except for ghee.

Shape the mixture into buffers.

Heat the ghee in a sizable pan and fry the buffers on both sides.

Serve while warm.

Chicory and Onion Omelet

The meal is a more fantastic choice for enjoyable breakfasts. When serving, consider additional toppings of onion salad or some simple tomatoes – they are the most significant sources of incorporating a hearty touch into the meal.

Servings: 2

Preparation time: 10 minutes

Ingredients:

- ¼ tsp. pepper
- 1 peeled and diced onion
- 1 tbsp. ghee
- 4 eggs
- 3 washed and halved chicory
- ½ bunch chives
- ¼ tsp. salt

Directions:

Heat the ghee in a pan and cook the chicory and onions in it. Turn occasionally.

Season the chicory with some salt and pepper.

Whisk the eggs and season properly with some salt and pepper.

Pour the egg mixture over the chicory and let it set with the lid closed. Then serve the omelet and garnish with chives.

Nut Bars

The nut bars are slightly different from the usual squares and come with a chewy and crispy texture that's fit for your mouth. The bars make a healthier breakfast and serve as a reliable snack or prepared in advance and added to the lunchbox pack.

Servings: 8

Preparation time: 15 minutes + 60 minutes refrigeration time

Ingredients:

- ¾ cup desiccated coconut
- ¼ cup hazelnuts
- ¾ cup dates
- ¼ cup melted coconut oil
- ¼ cup pumpkin seeds
- ¼ cup orange juice
- 1 cup pistachios

Directions:

Mix the pumpkin seeds with the pistachios, hazelnuts, dates, and desiccated coconut. Then mix with coconut oil and orange juice.

Layout the mixture and let it rest for 60 minutes in the refrigerator.

Then cut 8 bars out of it and serve.

Savory Bacon Muffins

This recipe is a perfect option for everyone who needs a delicious, moist, hearty meal. It is an excellent source of happiness for the family as it incorporates nutrition and sweetness through the specially selected ingredients.

Servings: 6

Preparation time: 20 minutes

Ingredients:

- 4 eggs
- ¼ tsp. salt
- 3 cherry tomatoes
- ¼ cup mushrooms
- 6 slices bacon
- ¼ tsp. pepper
- 1 small can washed and chopped chives

Directions:

Preheat the oven to 390°F.

Wash the tomatoes and mushrooms and cut them into small pieces.

Whisk the eggs with salt and pepper.

Put a slice of bacon in each of the muffin tins. Then add the egg mixture and chives.

Add tomatoes and mushrooms and bake the muffins for 10-15 minutes.

Hearty Burritos for Breakfast

Preparation of a burrito takes different approaches. However, this approach is for giving you the unique and hearty taste of a well-prepared burrito. It entails ingredients that are most commonly in the store, and therefore, you wouldn't strain a lot preparing this delicious delicacy.

Servings: 2

Preparation time: 14 minutes

Ingredients:

- ¼ cup chopped coriander
- ¼ cup cored and sliced red chili pepper
- ¼ tsp. pepper
- 4 separated eggs
- 1 cored and sliced avocado
- ¼ tsp. salt
- ½ cup fried meat
- 2 washed and diced tomatoes
- 1 cored and sliced red pepper
- ½ peeled and diced red onion
- 2 tbsp. olive oil

Directions:

Beat the egg whites until stiff.

Heat some oil in a sizable pan and add half of the egg white. Then let it boil and put it on a plate. Do the same with the remaining egg white.

Then heat the oil again in the same pan and steam the onion in it. Then add the vegetables (chili pepper, red pepper, and tomatoes), coriander, and meat.

Mix the egg yolks and add to the vegetables. Season the mixture with salt and pepper.

Top half the mixture with the egg white. Spread the avocado on top and roll it up carefully.

Stuffed Eggs

Stuffed eggs do well during holidays and camps but can as well work well for a proper breakfast. The recipe combines a few chosen and easily accessible ingredients such as avocado, coriander, chili powder, among other seasonings.

Servings: 12

Preparation time: 20 minutes

Ingredients:

- 1 tbsp. chopped hot peppers
- 1 tsp. diced red onion
- 6 eggs
- ¼ cup chili flakes
- 1 avocado
- ¼ tsp. salt
- 1 tbsp. cubed tomatoes
- ¼ tsp. chili powder
- 2 tsp. lime juice
- ¼ tsp. pepper
- 1 tbsp. chopped coriander

Directions:

Hard boil the eggs first, then quench and peel.

Halve the finished eggs and remove the yolks.

Stone the avocado and mash the pulp with the egg yolk. Then stir in the lime juice, coriander, onion, and hot peppers.

Season the mixture with salt and pepper. Then mix in the tomato cubes.

Pour the mixture into the eggs and garnish with chili flakes and chili powder.

Spinach Smoothie with Apple

Don't leave the Spinach smoothie with an apple of all the meals you should consider preparing at home. It is among the tastiest smoothies that incorporate ingredients crucial for your health. It is a perfect fit for a busy morning and, therefore, a great starter if you have more work over the day.

Servings: 2

Preparation time: 15 minutes

Ingredients:

- Juice of 1 lemon
- 1 peeled and cored apple
- 1 peeled and cored pear
- 2 handfuls spinach
- 1 cup water
- ½ tsp. ginger powder

Directions:

Puree the pear and apple.

Add the remaining set of ingredients and puree again.

Arrange the smoothie and let it cool in the refrigerator.

Quiche

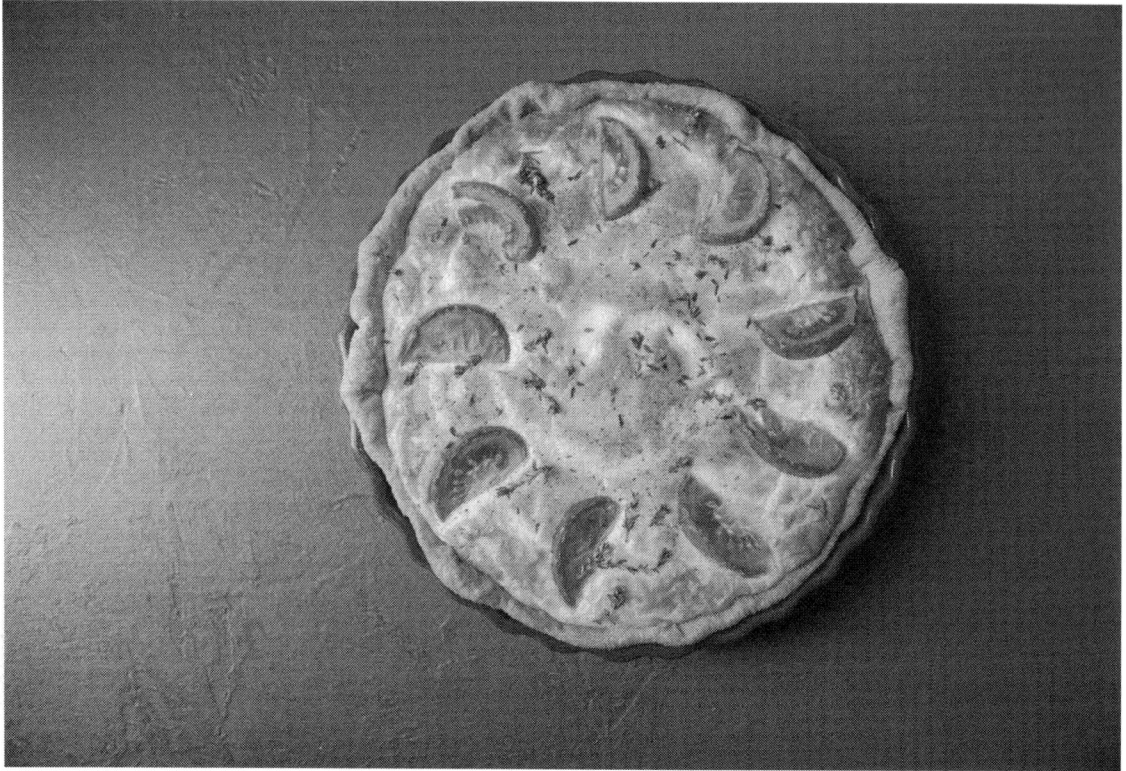

Preparation of a quiche might take a range of procedures. However, this approach of practice ensures that you experience the best out of quiche. It ensures that everyone in the family enjoys the best creamiest touch along with other tangible ingredients.

Servings: 1

Preparation time: 45 minutes

Ingredients:

For the dough:

- ½ tsp. salt
- 1 egg
- 2 tbsp. coconut oil
- 2 cups almond flour

For the filling:

- 1 cup sliced mushrooms
- 8 eggs
- 1 cup halved cherry tomatoes
- 1 tsp. salt
- ½ peeled and chopped onion
- 1 tsp. coconut oil
- 1 tsp. pepper
- 2 cups lettuce

Directions:

Work the flour with the egg, salt, and coconut oil into a dough.

Bakc the dough in a quiche pan at 350°F for 8-12 minutes. Mix the coconut oil with vegetables (mushrooms, tomatoes, onions, and lettuce) in the meantime.

Whisk the 8 eggs and season with salt and pepper.

Put the vegetables on the finished dough and pour the egg mixture over it. Then bake the quiche again for 30 minutes at 350°F.

Avocado Eggs

Preparing eggs alone may sound better but considering a piece or pieces of avocado will always incorporate healthiness into the dish. The avocado and other essential ingredients come loaded with fiber, fats, and oils crucial for body nourishment.

Servings: 2

Preparation time: 7 minutes

Ingredients:

- ¼ tsp. freshly ground black pepper
- 1 halved and pitted avocado
- 2 large eggs
- ¼ tsp. salt
- 2 tsp. avocado oil

Directions:

Cut a hole into each avocado half where the pit used to be.

In a sizable skillet, heat the oil over medium heat. Add the avocado halves and cook for 1 minute.

At the center of the halved avocado, crack an egg and cook to your desired doneness, 3 to 4 minutes.

Season with salt and pepper serving.

Mediterranean Egg Cups

You can always rely on the Mediterranean Egg Cups if you have a busy schedule ahead of you. It is one of the memorable meals packed with the sweetness and deliciousness you desire from simple and easily accessible ingredients. Enjoy the unique tastes on a bright morning as you prepare for a better day ahead.

Servings: 6

Preparation time: 25 minutes

Ingredients:

- 2 tbsp. sriracha
- A pinch of freshly ground black pepper
- 2 tbsp. diced tomatoes
- ½ tsp. dried oregano
- 2 tbsp. butter
- 1 tbsp. milk
- A dash salt
- 2 tbsp. sliced Kalamata olives
- 12 oz. drained and quartered artichoke hearts
- 8 large eggs
- 1 tbsp. crumbled feta cheese

Directions:

Preheat the oven to 350ºF. Grease a muffin tin with butter.

In a sizable bowl, mix together the eggs, milk, oregano, salt, and pepper.

Pour the mixture evenly into each muffin cup.

Distribute the tomatoes, olives, and artichoke hearts evenly into each muffin cup.

Bake until the eggs are set or for approximately 20 minutes.

Remove from the oven and top with feta cheese. Serve with Sriracha.

Breakfast Quinoa

For a proper and healthy breakfast, you require some quinoa. It is one of the best meals you'll meet with an appropriate combination of ingredients, including raspberries, almonds, and maple syrups to enhance the sweetness.

Servings: 2

Preparation time: 25 minutes

Ingredients:

- 2 tsp. slivered almonds
- ½ cup raspberries
- ¼ tsp. salt
- ¼ cup maple syrup
- 1 cup quinoa
- 2 cups coconut milk

Directions:

Put the quinoa in a medium bowl; rinse with cold water and drain. Transfer the quinoa to a small saucepan.

Add coconut milk and salt. Bring the quinoa to a rolling boil over medium-high heat.

Cover the sizable pan, and simmer (low heat) for 15 minutes.

Turn off the heat and leave the quinoa covered for 5 minutes. Uncover and transfer to two serving bowls.

Mix in the maple syrup.

Top with almonds and raspberries and serve.

Coconut and Almond Bars

One of the quickest meals to prepare for a delicious breakfast is this Coconut and almond bars recipe. It will help you save the morning hours of tedious meal preparations and adopt the entire family to a delicious and healthier meal schedule.

Servings: 16

Preparation time: 2 hours 20 minutes

Ingredients:

- ½ cup sunflower seeds
- 1 tsp. vanilla extract
- ½ cup pumpkin seeds
- ½ cup desiccated coconut
- 1 ¼ cups almond flour
- 1 pack baking powder
- ¼ cup raisins
- ¼ tsp. salt
- ¼ cup grapeseed oil
- ¼ cup almonds
- ¼ cup agave nectar

Directions:

Mix the almond flour with the baking powder and salt.

Mix the grapeseed oil with the vanilla and the nectar.

Add the mixture to the flour mixture and stir. Then mix in the raisins, desiccated coconut, almonds, pumpkin seeds, and sunflower seeds.

Then spread the dough on a baking sheet and bake for 20 minutes at 350°F.

Let the bars cool down for 2 hours.

Serve afterward.

Raspberry Smoothie

If you are a great lover of strawberry flavors, then this smoothie is a perfect choice. The sweetness in this smoothie is an exact fit for you. If you are in a hurry during the morning hours, you can consider this smoothie a perfect choice for a meal.

Servings: 2

Preparation time: 10 minutes

Ingredients:

- 1 cup almond milk
- 2 eggs
- 2 cups raspberries
- 2/3 cup desiccated coconut

Directions:

Wash and puree the raspberries.

Mix in the eggs, almond milk, and desiccated coconut.

Puree the smoothie again and serve.

Peach Relief Smoothie

If you want a starter that is quite friendly for your kids, you can always consider the Peach Relief smoothie. It is one of the most fantastic choices that will help your children grow nutritiously. It is easy to prepare, and therefore your kids can also learn to prepare them easily.

Servings: 1

Preparation time: 5 minutes

Ingredients:

- ½ cup fresh orange juice
- 2 halved, pitted and sliced fresh apricots
- ½ cup nut milk
- 1 cage-free egg
- 1 halved, pitted and frozen ripe peach

Directions:

Add all ingredients to a high-speed blender. Process until smooth, about 1 minute.

Pour into a large glass and serve immediately.

Morning Mellow Melon

Your morning should start with a refreshing meal. The morning mellow melon recipe is a proper instance of meals that start your morning with a vital encounter. It combines some of the essential fruits, including honeydew melon, grapefruit, and other essential ingredients. Keep enjoying it and even turn it into your best salad.

Servings: 1

Preparation time: 5 minutes

Ingredients:

- 2/3 cup thick coconut milk
- 1 cup sliced and frozen cantaloupe
- 4 tbsp. sweetener
- 1 cup sliced and frozen honeydew melon
- 1 grapefruit, juiced

Directions:

Add frozen honeydew chunks and grapefruit juice to a high-speed blender. Pulse to break down frozen honeydew.

Add the rest of the ingredients and process to smoothness, about 1 minute.

Pour into a large glass and serve immediately.

Guava Pop Smoothie

Another more excellent choice of a smoothie for breakfast is the Guava Pop Smoothie. It is also one of the greatest crowd pleasers and also a kid-friendly meal. It contains a set of ingredients that will always give you a hearty and delicious taste of a smoothie.

Servings: 1

Preparation time: 5 minutes

Ingredients:

- 2 juiced limes
- 1 cup coconut milk
- 1 pitted, peeled, diced and frozen mango
- 1 peeled and halved ripe guava
- ½ cup peeled, deseeded and sliced papaya

Directions:

Add coconut milk and guava to a high-speed blender. Process until smooth. Strain out seeds, reserving liquid.

Add strained guava mixture back to a high-speed blender with frozen mango chunks. Pulse to break down frozen mango.

Add rest of ingredients and process to smoothness, about 1 minute.

Pour into a large glass and serve immediately.

Lemon Freeze

If you desire to enjoy a perfect treat in the morning, it will help if you try this recipe. You can serve the Lemon Freeze at any time of the day.

Servings: 1

Preparation time: 5 minutes

Ingredients:

- ½ cup ice
- ½ cup fresh orange juice
- ½ cup coconut milk
- 4 tbsp. sweetener
- ½ cup fresh lemon juice

Directions:

Add ice and coconut milk to a high-speed blender. Pulse to crush ice.

Add the rest of the ingredients and process to smoothness, about 1 minute.

Pour into a large glass and serve immediately.

Peaches and Spiced Almonds

There is always that fabulous treat in almonds and peaches. A combination of both, along with a set of specially chosen spices, will always give you a unique crunch into a breakfast you've desired for some time. Add a few related toppings to enjoy more.

Servings: 1

Preparation time: 5 minutes

Ingredients:

- 1/8 tsp. vanilla
- ¼ tsp. ground ginger
- 4 dried pitted dates
- 1/3 cup raw almonds
- ¼ tsp. ground cinnamon
- 1/8 tsp. ground white pepper
- 2 halved, pitted and diced ripe peaches

Directions:

Add dates, almonds, vanilla, ginger, pepper, and cinnamon to a food processor or high-speed blender. Pulse to grind, about 1 minute coarsely.

Transfer the diced peaches to the serving dish.

Sprinkle on the almond mixture and serve immediately.

Cream of Cashew Cereal

It is one of the most excellent all-purpose meals with a savory touch and delicious taste fit for royalty. Enjoy it as you start the day.

Servings: 1

Preparation time: 5 minutes

Ingredients:

- ¼ tsp. Celtic sea salt
- 1 tbsp. raw honey
- ½ cup water
- 1 ½ cups soaked and drained raw cashews
- 1 peeled banana
- ¼ cup blueberries
- 1 tbsp. lemon juice
- ¼ tsp. vanilla

Directions:

Add the peeled banana to the food processor with soaked cashews, honey, lemon juice, vanilla, and salt.

Process until thick and fairly smooth, about 2 minutes.

Add enough water to reach desired consistency.

Transfer to serving dish and top with blueberries.

Serve immediately.

Very Berry Morning Mix

A combination of berries incorporates a range of flavors you desire for the mix. It is easy to prepare and doesn't eat up much of your time. Enjoy!

Servings: 1

Preparation time: 20 minutes

Ingredients:

- ¼ cup pitted cherries
- 1 small sprig of fresh mint
- ¼ cup blueberries
- 1 halved, pitted and diced nectarine
- ¼ cup blackberries
- ¼ cup raw nuts
- ½ inch piece peeled and minced fresh ginger
- ½ cup quartered strawberries

Directions:

Using a bowl, mix cherries, strawberries, ginger, nectarine, blackberries, and blueberries.

Chiffon mint leaves. Add to bowl and toss to combine. Transfer to serving dish.

Add nuts to a food processor and process properly to coarsely chop. Or add to paper or plastic kitchen bag and pound with a heavy rolling pin to crush.

Sprinkle on nuts and serve immediately or refrigerate for 20 minutes and serve chilled.

Main Dishes

The main dishes entail the best recipes specially chosen to ensure the lovers of a proper nutritional schedule enjoy the best. The dishes are easy to prepare, and the ingredients are easily available in the store.

Beef and Vegetable Stew

Beef and vegetable stew is an excellent pacesetter if you want to adapt to a healthy schedule. It entails simple preparation steps and specially chosen ingredients. You can always consider it as a main dish and enjoy it more.

Servings: 2

Preparation time: 20 minutes

Ingredients:

- 1 tbsp. turmeric
- ¼ tsp. salt
- 400 ml beef broth
- 1 peeled and chopped green onion
- 1 tbsp. cumin powder
- 3 peeled and diced carrots
- 1 cored and diced red pepper
- 1 tbsp. lard
- ¼ tsp. pepper
- 3 washed and diced stalks celery
- 400 g ground beef

Directions:

Heat the lard in a sizable saucepan and fry the onion in it. Season with turmeric and cumin.

Add the ground beef and fry. Add the vegetables (carrots, red pepper, and celery) and stir.

Deglaze with the broth and bring everything to a boil.

Let the stew simmer for 15 minutes.

Season with pepper and salt before serving.

Minced Beef and Pumpkin Soup

Minced beef and pumpkin soup are unique and easy to prepare. You can consider making the soup thicker to enjoy more.

Servings: 4

Preparation time: 35 minutes

Ingredients:

- 200 ml coconut milk
- 3 cloves garlic
- 1 peeled and diced butternut squash
- ¼ tsp. salt
- 1 peeled and chopped ginger
- 400 g minced meat
- 2 peeled and chopped onions
- 2 tbsp. coconut oil
- ¼ tsp. pepper
- 400 ml bone broth

Directions:

Heat 1 tbsp. coconut oil in a sizable saucepan and fry the onions, ginger, and garlic.

Add the squash and fry with it. Deglaze with the coconut milk and the broth and simmer for 20 minutes.

Puree the mixture and season the soup with salt and pepper. Then bring to the boil again.

Heat remaining 1 tbsp. coconut oil in a sizable pan and fry the minced meat. Season this with salt and pepper. Set the ready soup with the minced meat and serve.

Liver Dumpling

With a traditional origin, the meal comes with colorful flavors, especially in the soup. Prepare it in a day, and everyone in the family will keep yearning for it.

Servings: 12

Preparation time: 40 minutes

Ingredients:

- 1 peeled and chopped clove garlic
- 1 egg yolk
- ¼ tsp. pepper
- 1 handful washed and chopped parsley
- 2 lbs. bone broth
- ¼ tsp. salt
- 4 tbsp. arrowroot flour
- 1 peeled and chopped onion
- 250 g minced beef liver

Directions:

Mix onion and clove garlic with parsley, beef liver, egg yolk, and arrowroot flour.

Let the mixture rest in the refrigerator for 30 minutes. Heat the broth in a saucepan.

Form dumplings from the beef liver mass and add them to the broth. Then let it steep for 15 minutes.

As soon as the dumplings rise, drain, season with pepper and salt, and garnish with a little parsley.

Minced Beef and Vegetable Bowl

If you want to enjoy the filling taste of a properly prepared beef, you can always try this recipe. It also comes full of a range of vegetables that balance the nutrition ratio in the delicacy.

Servings: 2

Preparation time: 30 minutes

Ingredients:

For the minced meat:

- 1 tsp. paprika powder
- ½ tsp. chili powder
- ½ tsp. cumin
- ¼ tsp. salt
- 1 peeled clove garlic
- 300 g ground beef
- ¼ tsp. pepper
- 1 tsp. marjoram

For the vegetables:

- 2 tbsp. olive oil
- ¼ tsp. salt
- 2 handfuls endive
- 3 carrots
- ½ tsp. chili powder
- 3 parsnips

For the base:

- ¼ tsp. pepper
- 2 tbsp. kale pesto

Directions:

Preheat the oven to 390°F hot air.

Mix the beef with the spices.

Add the garlic to the minced meat through a garlic press.

Spread the mixture on half a baking sheet. Peel the vegetables and cut them into slices. Then mix the vegetables with spices and olive oil.

Spread the vegetable mixture next to the minced meat.

Cook both in the oven for 20-25 minutes. Switch on the grill function after 20 minutes.

Wash the endive salad and arrange it on plates.

Spread the minced meat and vegetables on top.

Garnish with pesto and pepper and serve.

Vegetable Roulades

If you are a great lover of vegetables, you can always enjoy the special vegetable filling by trying this particular recipe. It is quick and easy and comes with the best nutrients you desire. Enjoy!

Servings: 15

Preparation time: 45 minutes

Ingredients:

For the roulades:

- ¼ tsp. salt
- 5 sliced sun-dried tomatoes
- 1 tbsp. mustard
- ¼ tsp. pepper
- 1 handful washed and chopped parsley
- 1 egg
- 600 g minced beef
- 2 peeled and chopped cloves garlic
- 15 savoy cabbage leaves
- 1 tbsp. capers
- 1 peeled and chopped onions
- 2 tbsp. olive oil

For the sauce:

- 1 onion, peeled and chopped
- 2 tsps. paprika powder
- 400 ml bone broth
- 1 tbsp. tomato paste

Directions:

Slightly boil water and lower the temperature.

Then blanch the savoy cabbage leaves for 2 minutes. Put them off and place them to one side.

Mix the minced meat with 1 onion, garlic, tomatoes, and parsley. Then stir in the mustard, capers, egg, and spices.

Shape the minced meat mixture into dumplings and place them on the savoy cabbage leaves. Wind them up and fix them in place.

Heat the oil in a sizable pan and fry the roulades on all sides. Then take it out of the pan.

Peel and chop the other onion for sauce. Then sauté in the frying oil.

Stir in the paprika powder and tomato paste.

Deglaze with the broth and season with salt and pepper.

Add the roulades and simmer for 30 minutes with the cover closed.

Roast Pork with Mushrooms

Pork tastes better when roasted and works well when combined with adequately cooked mushrooms. It is a great combination that will introduce you to a healthy lifestyle. The roasted pork tastes beautiful, and the mushrooms are mouth-watering.

Servings: 5

Preparation time: 10 minutes

Ingredients:

- 200 g washed and quartered mushrooms
- 4 peeled and sliced shallots
- ¼ tsp. salt
- 800 g pork
- 2 tbsp. coconut oil
- 1 cup black tea
- 8 cored plums
- ¼ tsp. pepper

Directions:

Preheat the oven to 350°F.

Heat the coconut oil in a sizable pan and fry the meat on all sides.

Place the shallots, mushrooms, and plums in an ovenproof dish and season with salt and pepper.

Spread the meat on top and pour the tea over it. Close the dish with a lid and fry for 1.5 hours. Then remove the meat and puree the sauce.

Serve both together.

Spicy Veal Liver

Veal liver along with specially chosen spices is quite a fantastic meal. Enjoy!

Servings: 2

Preparation time: 10 minutes

Ingredients:

- 1 apple
- ¼ tsp. pepper
- 3 tbsp. bone broth
- 2 veal liver
- 1 peeled and sliced onion
- ¼ tsp. salt
- 2 tbsp. coconut oil
- 1 bunch Swiss chard, washed and leaves separated

Directions:

Heat some coconut oil in a sizable pan and roast the onion in it. Then deglaze with the bone broth.

Add some coconut oil to a separate pan and fry the chard in it. Then add the leaves and fry them.

Season the chard with salt and pepper. Then cook with the lid closed.

In the meantime, core and dice the apple. Add the apple to the chard. Fry the veal liver on both sides.

Place the fried onions on top and let cook with the lid closed.

Arrange the chard and drape the liver on top.

Garnish with the fried onions and serve.

Classic Boiled Beef

Frying beef or roasting it is a more excellent option, but you can also prepare the meat by boiling it classically. Boiled beef also follows a traditional origin and comes with a more tender and softer touch than you'd experience with the roasted version. Enjoy!

Servings: 2

Preparation time: 2 hours 15 minutes

Ingredients:

- 2 liters water
- 1 onion
- 2 bay leaves
- 1 leek
- 2 parsnips
- 500 g boiled beef
- 3 peeled and sliced carrots
- 5 juniper berries
- 100 g celeriac
- 2 tsp. salt

For the horseradish:

- 1 tbsp. lemon juice
- 2 tbsp. freshly grated horseradish
- 1 grated apple
- A dash salt

Directions:

Slightly boil the water before adding salt.

Add the onion with the juniper berries, and the bay leaves to the water. Then add the boiled beef and simmer for 2 hours.

Add the vegetables to the meat after 1.5 hours and cook.

Mix the apple with horseradish, salt, and lemon juice. Drain the vegetables and meat.

Remove the onion, bay leaves, and juniper berries.

Cut the boiled beef into slices.

Serve the meat with the vegetables and the horseradish.

Cauliflower with Bacon

Cauliflower with bacon is also a great recipe you can always consider as a main meal. It entails a combination of ingredients that are easily accessible and fit for your health. Enjoy!

Servings: 4

Preparation time: 60 minutes

Ingredients:

- 1 peeled and chopped onion
- 2 tbsp. ground almonds
- 1 cauliflower (stalk and leaves removed)
- 600 g ground beef
- 250 g bacon
- ¼ tsp. salt and pepper
- 1 egg
- 2 peeled and chopped cloves garlic
- 1 tsp. paprika spice

Directions:

Preheat the oven to 350°F.

Cook the cauliflower in salted water for 10 minutes.

Fry the beef with garlic, egg, almonds, and onions. Season the minced meat with paprika, pepper, and salt.

Put the cauliflower on a sizable baking tray and spread the minced meat over it.

Spread the bacon over the minced meat and bake the mixture for 40 minutes.

Meatloaf

The approach of preparing this meatloaf is relatively quick and easy, and therefore, you will not strain with the procedures. Again, the ingredients are simple and easily accessible. Enjoy the perfect outcome of this recipe!

Servings: 3

Preparation time: 60 minutes

Ingredients:

- 2 tbsp. pine nuts
- 1 handful basil
- 600 g minced meat
- 1 egg
- 2 tsp. paprika powder
- 1 tbsp. potato starch
- 2 tsp. mustard
- ¼ tsp. salt and pepper
- 2 peeled and chopped cloves garlic
- 1 peeled and chopped onion
- 3 stalks parsley
- 6 sliced sun-dried tomatoes
- 3 sprigs of lemon thyme
- 1 peeled and grated potato

Directions:

Preheat the oven to 350°F.

Mix the entire set of ingredients together.

Shape the mass into a loaf. Grease a baking pan and add the minced meat mixture.

Close the form with a lid and bake the meatloaf for 50 minutes.

Eggplant with Minced Meat Filling

The recipe gives you an exceptional meat-filling taste along with the delicious touch of the eggplant in a meal. With the inclusion of a few seasonings and spices, the dish is fit for a king.

Servings: 2

Preparation time: 35 minutes

Ingredients:

- 1 washed and chopped sprig rosemary
- ½ (8 oz.) can chunkily tomatoes
- 2 tbsp. coconut oil
- ¼ tsp. salt and pepper
- 2 eggplants
- 300 g minced meat
- 1 peeled and chopped clove garlic
- 1 tsp. paprika spice
- 1 halved aubergine

Directions:

Preheat the oven to 350°F.

Heat 1 tbsp. coconut oil in a sizable pan and fry the aubergines in it. Then put in a baking dish.

Heat the remaining coconut oil again in the same pan and fry the minced meat in it. Then add the aubergine pulp and the garlic.

Stir in the tomatoes, eggplants, and rosemary.

Season the mixture accordingly with paprika, salt, and pepper.

Pour the minced meat mixture into the aubergines and bake for 20 minutes.

Leek Soup with Minced Meat

You can always enjoy minced meat if you have a good soup with you. Leek soup works as a perfect choice and comes loaded with a range of ingredients that generate a flavorful meal. Enjoy with friends and family!

Servings: 4

Preparation time: 10 minutes

Ingredients:

- 80 g sliced beef jerky
- 1½ liter vegetable stock
- ½ bunch washed and sliced spring onions and leek
- 350 g minced meat
- ½ tsp. nutmeg
- ¼ tsp. salt and pepper
- 4 leek sticks
- 3 tbsp. coconut milk
- 2 tbsp. olive oil

Directions:

Heat the olive oil in a sizable saucepan and fry the minced meat in it. Then add the beef jerky and fry.

Then add the spring onions and the leek.

Deglaze with the vegetable stock and let the soup simmer for 15 minutes.

Finally, stir in the coconut milk.

Before serving, season with salt, pepper, and nutmeg.

Salmon with Avocado Mousse

If you want to enjoy the salmon, choose the avocado mousse and other essential ingredients as an option. Like any other sweet meal, the delicious meal boasts a range of nutritious ingredients crucial for your health. Enjoy!

Servings: 4

Preparation time: 15 minutes

Ingredients:

- 1 washed and chopped spring onion
- 200 g smoked salmon
- ½ peeled and diced cucumber
- 1 tbsp. dill
- 3 cored and hollowed avocados
- ½ tbsp. lemon juice
- 1 handful cress
- ¼ tsp. salt and pepper

Directions:

Mix the avocado mousse with the cucumber, spring onion, cress, and lemon juice. Then season with salt and pepper.

Wash and chop the dill.

Dice the salmon.

Mix both and season with salt and paper.

Arrange the salmon with the avocado pulp and serve.

Cod with White Cabbage

White cabbage serves as a better partner for seafood like cod. It comes with one of the unique tastes everyone desires to enjoy.

Servings: 2

Preparation time: 45 minutes

Ingredients:

- 4 tbsp. olive oil
- 2 cod fillets
- 1 washed and wedged white cabbage
- 2 tbsp. spring onions
- ¼ tsp. salt and pepper

For the sauce:

- 1 tsp. apple cider vinegar
- 2 tbsp. mustard
- ½ tsp. honey
- ¼ tsp. pepper
- 1 ½ tsps. lemon juice

Directions:

Preheat your oven to 350°F.

Spread the cabbage and onions on a prepared baking sheet and drizzle over with the olive oil. Season with pepper and salt.

Bake the cabbage for 40 minutes.

Mix all the ingredients for the sauce.

Season the fish with salt and pepper and fry it on both sides.

Arrange the cabbage with the sauce and the fish and serve.

Salsa Salmon

Salmon is one of the most excellent choices of ingredients anyone would wish to enjoy. However, a few additional elements, such as coriander and red onion, give a different taste everyone desires to enjoy. Try it and enjoy it the best.

Servings: 2

Preparation time: 10 minutes + 30 minutes refrigeration time

Ingredients:

- 1 tsp. paprika powder
- 2 tbsp. chopped coriander
- 1 tsp. pepper
- 1 tsp. salt
- 1 cored and sliced avocado
- 1 tsp. onion powder
- 2 salmon fillets
- 1 cored and diced red pepper
- ¼ tsp. chili powder
- 2 tbsp. olive oil
- Juice 2 limes
- 1 peeled and diced red onion

Directions:

Mix the olive oil with paprika and onion powder.

Using your hand, rub the salmon with olive oil and let it stand in the refrigerator for 30 minutes.

Mix the red onion with the avocado, red pepper, coriander, and lime juice. Then season to taste with pepper, salt, olive oil, and chili powder.

Fry the salmon in a pan and serve with the salsa.

Curry Prawns

You can always enjoy the best by trying this recipe. Curry prawns will always give you the best seafood taste and a perfect touch out of curry. Enjoy!

Servings: 12

Preparation time: 10 minutes

Ingredients:

- 2 egg whites
- ½ tsp. curry powder
- 2 tbsp. olive oil
- ¼ tsp. salt and pepper
- 380 g prawns with shell
- 2 diced shallots
- Juice and zest of half a lime
- 10 g diced ginger
- 1 diced red chili pepper
- 1 diced clove garlic
- 1 bunch chopped coriander
- 500 ml coconut milk
- 1 tsp. red curry paste

Directions:

Heat olive oil in a sizable pan.

Steam the garlic, chili pepper, shallots, and ginger in it. Then stir in the curry paste and let the mixture cool down.

Puree 100 g prawns with the egg white and salt.

Chop the remaining prawns and mix with the ginger mixture and coriander.

Form patties from the shrimp mixture.

Heat the rest of the olive oil in a sizable pan and fry the patties on all sides.

Mix the coconut milk with the lime juice as well as the lime zest and the curry powder. Season with salt and pepper.

Arrange the prawns and serve with the dip.

Chocolate Strawberry Cupcakes

Enjoy the flavor from fresh strawberry and chocolate in these cupcakes. The sweetness in this meal is entirely designed for you.

Servings: 12

Preparation time: 15 minutes

Ingredients:

- ½ cup warm water
- 1 tsp. xanthan gum
- 1 ½ tsp. baking soda
- ½ cup sorghum flour
- ½ cup whole milk
- ¼ tsp. sea salt
- 1 cup fresh strawberries
- 1/3 cup tapioca flour
- ½ tsp. baking powder
- ½ cup millet flour
- ¼ cup unsweetened cocoa powder
- 3 tbsp. canola oil
- 2 beaten large eggs
- 1 tsp. vanilla extract
- 1/3 cup potato starch

Directions:

Set your oven to preheat to 350°F and line a muffin pan with paper liners.

Combine the salt, baking powder, baking soda, xanthan gum, cocoa powder, potato starch, and the flours (sorghum, tapioca, and millet), then add to a mixing bowl.

Whisk together the water, eggs, milk, vanilla extract, and canola oil.

Combine both containers of ingredients – beat on high speed for 2 minutes.

Mash your strawberries gently with a fork. Fold the strawberries into the batter.

Spoon the batter into the pan evenly.

Bake until done (about 20 minutes)

Cool the cupcakes completely.

Top with icing and extra strawberries.

Orange Squares

Don't miss orange flavors in your main meals. The orange squares will always give you an enchanting experience with meals. You can enjoy it along with other crucial meals.

Servings: 8

Preparation time: 25 minutes

Ingredients:

For the Crust Layer:

- 5 pitted medjool dates
- ¼ cup unsweetened shredded coconut
- ¼ tsp. salt
- ¾ cup chopped almonds
- 2 ½ tsp. fresh orange zest

For the Top Layer:

- 3 drops liquid stevia
- 2 tbsp. honey
- 1 tsp. fresh orange zest
- 1/3 cup coconut oil
- 2 tbsp. fresh orange juice

Directions:

In a food processor, combine the almonds, coconut, dates, salt, and orange zest for the crust layer until well combined.

Transfer into the bottom of a square glass dish that has been lined with parchment paper, spreading evenly.

Beat the coconut oil in a mixing bowl until creamy.

Add the orange juice, orange zest, honey, and liquid stevia and blend until smooth.

Spread the mixture over the crust layer, then cover with plastic and chill for 2 hours or until set.

Remove the parchment paper and cut it into squares.

Serve cold topped with a shake of icing sugar or coconut.

Sicilian Salad

If you desire a simple, easy, gluten-free meal, the salad is a more fantastic choice. It comes loaded with the essential ingredients and ensures proper nutrition and body growth among kids.

Servings: 3

Preparation time: 10 minutes

Ingredients:

- 3 tbsp. olive oil
- 1 clove minced garlic
- 1 juiced lemon
- ¼ tsp. red pepper flakes
- 1 bunch Lacinato kale
- ½ tsp. dried oregano
- ¼ tsp. sea salt
- 1 tsp. ground black pepper

Topping:

- ¼ cup green olives
- ½ lb. diced hard salami
- ½ cup roasted cauliflower
- ½ cup pickled sweet peppers
- 6 marinated artichoke hearts
- ¼ cup toasted sunflower seeds
- 6 pickled red onion slices rings
- ½ cup pepperoncini

Directions:

Combine your salt, pepper, oregano, olive oil, garlic, lemon juice, and red pepper flakes.

Close with the lid and blend it by shaking vigorously.

Slice kale leaves thinly and toss them in a bowl.

Coat kale with the lemon dressing.

Combine the topping ingredients.

Place kale in individual salad bowls.

Sprinkle topping over the kale and serve.

Enjoy!

White Chocolate Chip Cookies

The meal is a set of fresh cookies where everyone can enjoy the deliciousness. Feel free to incorporate a few sweeter ingredients.

Servings: 12

Preparation time: 40 minutes

Ingredients:

- 3 tsp. vanilla extract
- 1 cup sorghum flour
- ¾ cup potato starch
- 1 ½ cups packed brown sugar
- ¾ cup semisweet white chocolate chips
- ½ cup almond flour
- ½ tsp. salt
- 1 tsp. xanthan gum
- 2/3 cup canola oil
- 1 tsp. baking soda
- 2 large eggs

Directions:

Combine your dry ingredients in a bowl.

Whisk your vanilla, eggs, and oil in a separate bowl, then beat into the dry ingredients until smooth and well combined.

Fold in the white chocolate chips, then cover and chill the dough for 45 to 60 minutes.

Set the oven to preheat to 350°F and line a baking sheet with foil.

Shape the dough into 1-inch balls and arrange them on the baking sheet.

Lightly flatten each cookie and bake for 12 to 14 minutes, turning halfway, until golden on the edges but still soft to the touch.

Let the cookies cool in the pan for 3 to 5 minutes, then allow to cool completely. Enjoy.

Garlic Aioli

Enjoy the garlicky flavor like never before. It entails simple preparation steps and will make you prepare more.

Servings: ½ cup

Preparation time: 10 minutes

Ingredients:

- 2 tbsp. extra-virgin olive oil
- 1/3 cup canola oil
- 1 egg yolk
- 1 small minced garlic clove
- 1 tsp. lemon juice

Directions:

Whisk the garlic, lemon juice, and egg yolk until integrated.

Whisking constantly, slowly drizzle in the olive oil a few drops at a time.

Continue to whisk constantly to emulsify, slowly drizzle in the canola oil a few drops at a time until thick and pale.

Refrigerate, covered, for up to 3 days.

Serve and enjoy!

Cinnamon Rice Crispy Treats

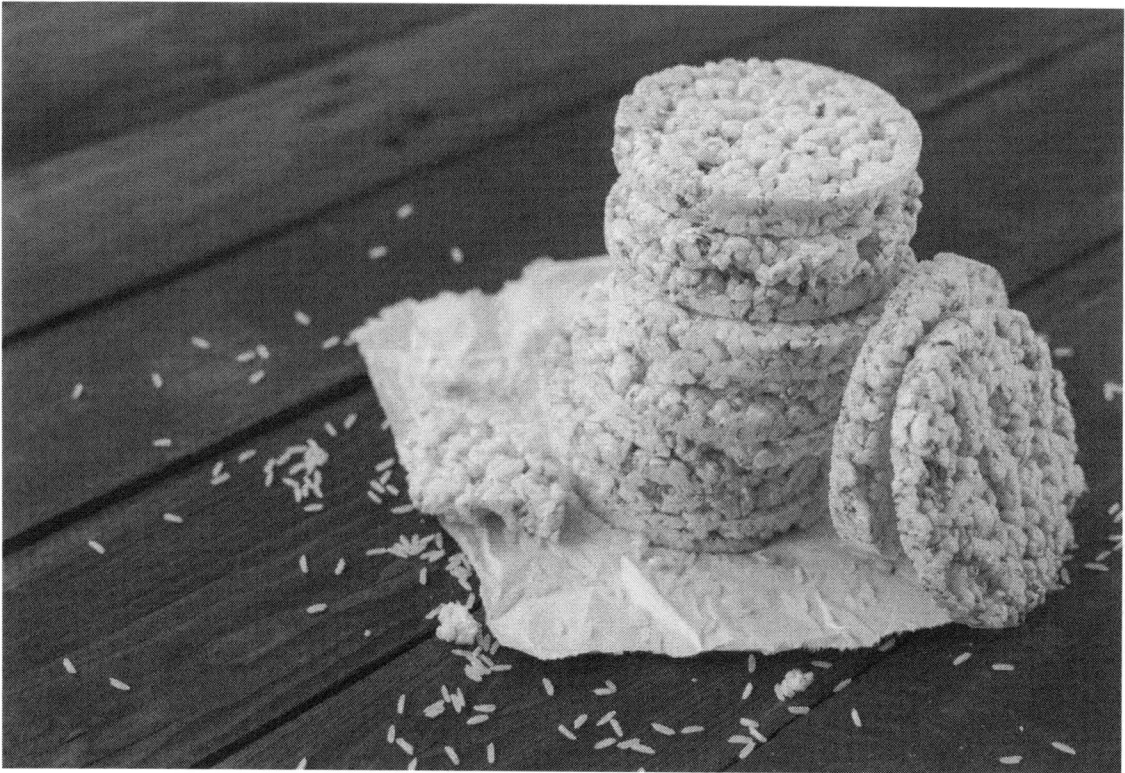

A perfect choice of ingredients lies at the center of this recipe. A few sweeter ingredients ensure to incorporate a taste like never before. Enjoy!

Servings: 6

Preparation time: 10 minutes

Ingredients:

- 1 ½ tsp. vanilla extract
- 6 cups gluten-free rice cereal
- ½ cup agave nectar
- ¾ cup natural almond butter
- 2 tbsp. coconut oil
- 1 tbsp. cinnamon powder

Directions:

Line the baking pan and set it aside.

Add the agave nectar and cinnamon powder to a saucepan on medium heat, stir, allow to melt, and bubble slowly.

Switch off the heat, then stir in your vanilla extract, coconut oil, and almond butter.

Stir the mixture gently until it thickens slightly.

Pour the cereal into a large bowl, then top with your agave mixture.

Gently stir the cereal until it is evenly coated, then press it into the prepared pan, spreading it evenly.

Cover the pan with plastic and chill until the bars are firm.

Cut to serve.

Rosemary Crackers

You'll always start by enjoying the fine and sweet rosemary aroma. Don't forget to prepare enough and extras for your friends.

Servings: 12

Preparation time: 15 minutes

Ingredients

- 1 tbsp. olive oil
- 1 egg white
- 2 tbsp. water
- ¼ tsp. coconut oil
- 2 cups almond flour
- 2 tbsp. rosemary
- ½ tsp. sea salt

Directions:

Preheat oven to 350°F.

Combine salt, almond flour and rosemary in a medium bowl.

Combine the coconut oil, water, olive oil, and egg white and whisk them together.

Transfer the egg mixture to the flour mixture then stir until a dough forms.

Add water or oil only if it doesn't stick together as a dough ball.

Roll dough between parchment paper to an even thickness of ¼ inch thick.

Add the parchment to a baking pan then discard the top parchment.

Bake for 10 minutes, let them settle in the oven for 10 minutes with the heat turned off.

Great when served with Hummus.

Enjoy!

Almond Butter Cookies

The Almond Butter Cookies take more straightforward preparation steps and include easily accessible ingredients among all the cookies. The cookies are tasty and sweet. Enjoy!

Servings: 12

Preparation time: 30 minutes

Ingredients:

- 1 large egg
- 1 cup smooth natural almond butter
- ¾ cup white sugar
- 1 tsp. baking soda
- 1 pinch salt
- ½ tsp. vanilla extract

Directions:

Preheat to the oven to 350°F and line a baking pan.

Beat together the sugar, baking soda, vanilla extract, salt, and egg in a mixing bowl until smooth.

Add the almond butter and beat until well combined.

Drop the dough in rounded teaspoons onto the prepared baking sheet and lightly flatten with the back of a fork.

Bake for 10 minutes, turning halfway, or until the cookies are just set.

Leave on the tray to set for 10 minutes, then cool and serve.

Crunchy Pineapple Cinnamon Flips

The flavor of pineapple and cinnamon is quite impressive. A combination of other ingredients adds up to the flavors to make everything more delicious. Enjoy!

Servings: 6

Preparation time: 2 hours 10 minutes

Ingredients

- 2 pineapples
- 1 tsp. cinnamon

Directions:

Preheat oven to 200°F.

Slice the pineapple into very thin slices.

Line the slices on a baking sheet covered in parchment paper. Leave space between the slices.

Sprinkle with cinnamon.

Bake the slices for 1 hour, then flip them over.

Continue baking and flipping for 1-2 hours until they're dry throughout.

Cool them and enjoy.

Quinoa Stuffed Peppers

The meal is a pack of proteins in bell pepper and a good choice for the entire family. You can enjoy it more when you prepare it during the weekends or weeknight dinners.

Servings: 4

Preparation time: 55 minutes

Ingredients:

- 3 minced garlic cloves
- 6 yellow bell peppers
- 2 tbsp. nonstick cooking spray
- 1 peeled and diced carrot
- ½ cup tri-color quinoa
- ¼ tsp. freshly ground black pepper
- 1 cup water
- 2 tbsp. coconut oil
- ½ diced small onion
- 12 oz. diced firm tofu
- ¼ tsp. salt

Directions:

Preheat the oven to 350°F.

Grease a sizable baking dish with nonstick cooking spray.

Rinse the quinoa in a fine-mesh strainer until the water runs clear.

Put the quinoa in a sizeable saucepan, add the water, boil for about 10 minutes or until the water is absorbed.

Remove from heat and cover the saucepan.

In a sizable skillet, heat the coconut oil over medium-high heat.

Add the carrot, onion, tofu, and garlic. Sauté for approximately 5 minutes, or until the vegetables are soft. Season generously with salt and black pepper.

Adjust the heat to high, add the cooked quinoa, and stir for an additional 1 to 2 minutes. Remove from the heat.

Cut off the bell pepper tops and remove the seeds. Spoon the quinoa and vegetable mixture into the peppers.

Place the stuffed peppers into the prepared baking dish and bake for 25 to 30 minutes.

Set the stuffed peppers aside from the oven and let sit for 5 minutes before serving.

Hawaiian Tofu Kabobs

The dish is easier and requires a few easy-to-access ingredients. Surprisingly, the outcome is delicious and will ensure everyone yearns for it every time.

Servings: 4

Preparation time: 1 hour 15 minutes

Ingredients:

- 2 sliced red bell peppers
- 10 oz. gluten-free hoisin sauce
- 12 oz. firm tofu chunks
- ¼ cup sesame oil
- 20 oz. pineapple chunks

Directions:

Put the tofu chunks into a medium bowl.

Put the peppers and pineapple in a separate medium bowl.

In a sizable bowl, mix the hoisin and sesame oil.

Top half of the mixture over the tofu and half over the pineapple and peppers, tossing to coat the ingredients with the sauce. Cover the bowls, set them in a refrigerator.

Marinate for at least 1 hour.

Preheat the oven to 425°F.

To make the kabobs, alternate ingredients on metal skewers and place them on a parchment-lined sheet pan. Bake for 15 minutes. Serve warm.

Roasted Cauliflower and Chickpea Tacos

When roasted, cauliflower combined with chickpea tacos and other ingredients gives the best feeling and enjoyment ever. Try it and enjoy!

Servings: 4

Preparation time: 25 minutes

Ingredients:

- 1 chopped celery stalk
- 15 oz. strained, liquid reserved and divided chickpeas
- 2 tbsp. Sriracha
- 1 tbsp. tomato paste
- ¼ tsp. freshly ground black pepper
- 8 corn tortillas or taco shells
- 1 peeled and chopped carrot
- 14 oz. sliced frozen cauliflower
- 1 tbsp. Dijon mustard
- 2 tsp. olive oil
- 4 minced garlic cloves
- 1 chopped small onion
- ¼ tsp. salt
- 2 tbsp. apple cider vinegar

Directions:

Put the frozen cauliflower in a strainer in the sink and run cold water over the cauliflower to defrost.

In a small bowl, whisk together ¼ cup of reserved chickpea liquid with the Sriracha, vinegar, tomato paste, and mustard.

In a separate small bowl, mash ½ cup of chickpeas.

Add the seasoned liquid to the mashed chickpeas and set aside.

In a sizable skillet, heat the oil over medium heat.

Add the carrot, garlic, celery, and onion and sauté for about 3 minutes or soften the vegetables.

Add the mashed chickpea mixture and the remaining chickpeas to the skillet and stir for about 1 minute, or until they're heated through.

Turn off the heat and season the mixture with salt and pepper.

Layer the mixture inside corn tortillas or taco shells, and top as desired.

Chickpea Curry with Kale

Regardless of your perception of curry, this recipe will instill the desire to enjoy chickpea curry daily. When prepared along with kale, you will enjoy the nutritious touch.

Servings: 4

Preparation time: 40 minutes

Ingredients:

For the spice blend:

- ½ tsp. cayenne pepper
- 1 tsp. coriander, ground
- 1 tsp. sea salt
- 1 tsp. cumin, ground
- 1 tsp. ground turmeric

For the curry:

- 8 oz. diced tomatoes
- 1 finely chopped small red onion
- 2 minced garlic cloves
- 1 tsp. coconut oil
- 1 diced medium sweet potato
- 1-inch peeled and minced piece fresh ginger
- ½ cup full-fat coconut cream
- ½ cup vegetable stock or water
- 5 oz. rinsed and drained chickpeas
- 3 cups stemmed and chopped fresh kale

Directions:

To make the spice blend

In a sizable bowl, combine the cumin, turmeric, coriander, salt, and cayenne pepper. Mix well.

To make the curry

In another sizable skillet, heat the oil over medium heat.

Add the onion and cook for 3 minutes, or until fragrant and translucent.

Add the sweet potato and stir properly to cook for 2 more minutes.

Add ginger, garlic, and spice blend, and cook for another 30 seconds.

Add the coconut cream, tomatoes with their juices, and stock, then stir to combine.

Cover and cook over high heat, bringing the curry to a low boil.

Add the chickpeas before lowering the heat and simmer for approximately 20 minutes, or until the sweet potato is tender.

Set aside from heat and stir in the kale before serving.

Mexican Salmon Burgers

You can always eat the burgers as they are or even enjoy them with your favorite side dish.

Servings: 4

Preparation time: 40 minutes

Ingredients:

For the burgers:

- ½ seeded and chopped poblano pepper
- ¼ tsp. freshly ground black pepper
- 1 tbsp. freshly squeezed lemon
- ½ cup almond flour
- 2 chopped scallions
- ½ tsp. salt
- ¼ lb. skinned and chopped salmon fillets
- 1 large egg

For the avocado salsa:

- ¼ tsp. salt
- ¼ tsp. freshly ground black pepper
- 1 chopped large ripe avocado
- 2 chopped scallions
- 1 tbsp. freshly squeezed lemon juice
- ½ seeded and chopped poblano pepper

Directions:

To make the burgers:

Put the chopped salmon into a large bowl.

Add the almond flour, egg, scallions, poblano pepper, lemon juice, salt, and pepper to the salmon, and mix well.

Form the salmon mixture into 4 patties.

Set an indoor grill pan or outdoor grill on medium-high heat.

Cook each burger for about 4 minutes on each side, or until cooked through.

Top the burgers with salsa before serving.

To make the avocado salsa:

Add the avocado, poblano pepper, scallions, lemon juice, salt, and pepper in a medium bowl. Mix well.

Set aside on the counter if using within 30 minutes.

Store covered in the refrigerator if you are preparing it ahead of time.

Roasted Cod and Sweet Potatoes

The seafood taste from the cod and several sweet potatoes is impressive. You can prepare it, and the entire family will enjoy it more.

Servings: 4

Preparation time: 45 minutes

Ingredients:

- 1 tsp. freshly ground black pepper
- 1 thinly sliced lemon
- ¼ cup olive oil, plus more for drizzling
- 1 tsp. salt
- 4 minced garlic cloves
- 2 peeled and thinly sliced large sweet potatoes
- 6 oz. cod fillets

Directions:

Preheat the oven to 425°F.

Line a sheet pan with parchment paper.

In a sizable bowl, toss the sweet potatoes with the oil, garlic, salt, and pepper.

Place the sweet potatoes on the sheet pan in two even rows, to make a bed for the fish.

Bake the sweet potatoes for 30 minutes.

Set aside and put the cod fillets on top of the sweet potatoes. Drizzle with oil and top with lemon slices.

Bake them until the fish flakes with a fork or for approximately 15 minutes.

Serve warm.

Potato Chip-Crusted Salmon

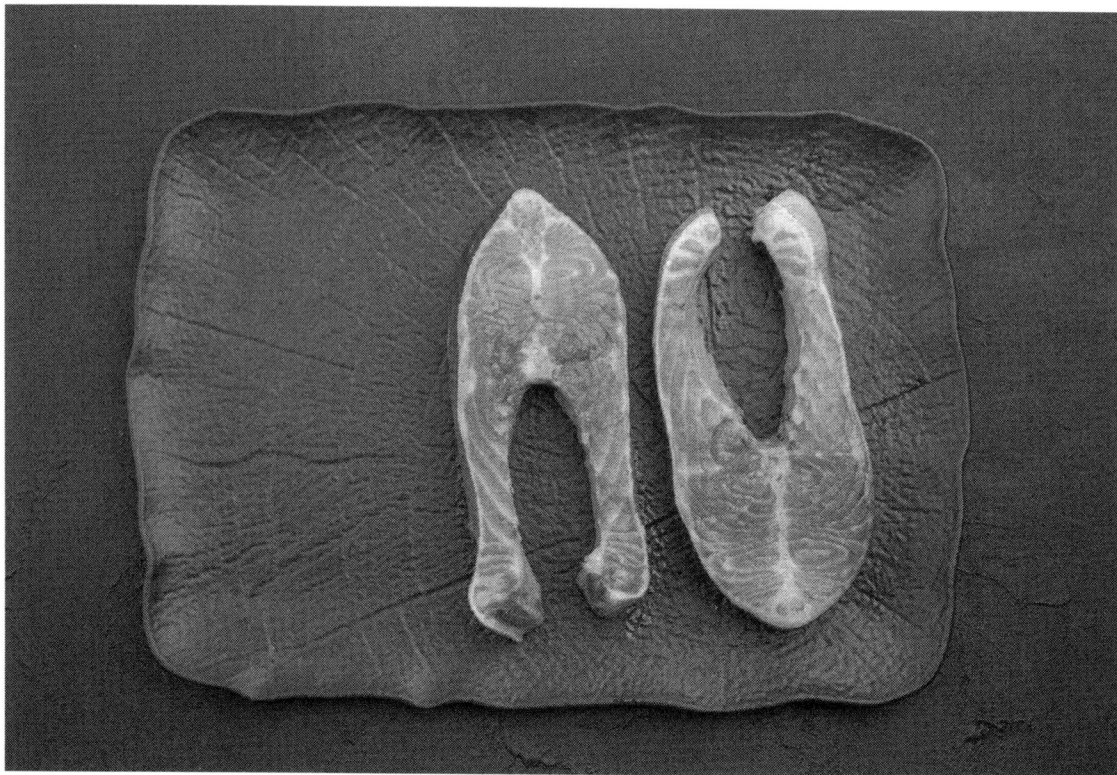

The dish helps save time in the kitchen, and the outcome is something delicious for friends and the entire family. Enjoy!

Servings: 4

Preparation time: 20 minutes

Ingredients:

- ¼ tsp. freshly ground black pepper
- 6 oz. salmon fillets
- 4 tbsp. divided Dijon mustard
- ¼ tsp. salt
- 5 oz. salt and vinegar potato chips

Directions:

Preheat the oven to 450°F.

Place the salmon fillets in a shallow 9-by-13-inch baking dish lined with parchment paper.

Smash potato chips in a resealable bag.

Spread a tablespoon of the mustard over each fish fillet and season with salt and pepper.

Top each fillet evenly with the crushed potato chips.

Bake the fish flakes properly with a fork or for approximately 15 minutes.

Serve and enjoy.

Roasted Olive Chicken

Preparing a tasty chicken can be a bit trickier. However, you can always try a different version of roasting in olive oil along with essential ingredients. Enjoy!

Servings: 4

Preparation time: 20 minutes

Ingredients:

- ¼ tsp. freshly ground black pepper
- 2 lbs. bone-in chicken
- ½ tsp. garlic powder
- 1 tsp. paprika
- 2 sliced lemons
- 1 chopped sweet onion
- 3 tbsp. olive oil
- 15 oz. rinsed and drained pitted green olives
- ½ tsp. salt

Directions:

Preheat the oven to 400°F.

Arrange the chicken, olives, lemon slices, and onion on a sheet pan.

In a sizable bowl, mix the oil with paprika, salt, garlic powder, and pepper.

Evenly coat the chicken, olives, lemon slices, and onion with the oil mixture.

Roast until the chicken achieves an internal temperature of 165°F or approximately 45 minutes. Let the chicken rest for around 5 minutes, then serve.

Crispy Fried Chicken Cutlets

It is among the most incredible meals no one will turn down. Enjoy and ensure to keep more for enjoying in later moments when hunger strikes again.

Servings: 4

Preparation time: 20 minutes

Ingredients:

- ½ cup potato starch
- 2 tbsp. flavor-neutral oil
- 1 tsp. paprika
- 1 cup chickpea flour
- 1 tsp. garlic powder
- ¼ tsp. salt
- 2 large eggs
- 2 lbs. chicken cutlets
- 1 tsp. Sriracha
- ¼ tsp. freshly ground black pepper
- 1 tsp. onion powder
- 1 tsp. gluten-free soy sauce
- ½ tsp. dried parsley

Directions:

Season the chicken with salt and pepper. In a sizable bowl, mix together the eggs, soy sauce, and Sriracha.

Mix the flour, potato starch, onion powder, garlic powder, paprika, and parsley in a medium bowl.

Line a large plate with paper towels and a second large plate with parchment paper.

Coat each chicken cutlet first in the egg mixture, followed by the flour mixture.

Place each cutlet on the parchment-covered plate, repeating until all of the cutlets are coated.

Heat the oil on a sizable skillet over medium heat. Fry the cutlets for about 4 minutes per side or until golden brown and cooked through without overcrowding the pan.

Place the finished cutlets on the paper towel-lined plate to absorb the excess oil, then serve.

Desserts

Desserts provide the best option for a healthy lifestyle. The desserts in this section are simple and don't take much preparation time. Enjoy them.

Meringue Cookies

The cookies are naturally gluten-free and sweet. Enjoy them.

Servings: 12

Preparation time: 35 minutes

Ingredients:

- ½ tsp. vanilla extract
- 1 tsp. white vinegar
- ¼ tsp. salt
- ½ cup sugar
- 2 egg whites
- ½ tsp. cream of tartar

Directions:

Preheat the oven to 225°F.

Line a sheet pan with parchment paper.

Beat the egg whites properly with the cream of tartar and salt, with the help of a hand mixer to form soft peaks. Let them face up when the mixer is lifted.

Add the sugar gradually, continuing to beat until stiff peaks form.

Fold in the vinegar and vanilla extract.

Place teaspoon-sized dollops of the mixture on the prepared pan.

Bake the mixture for 25 minutes.

Turn off the oven, and let the meringues cool in the oven before serving.

Peanut Butter Chocolate Chip Cookies

Prepare the peanut butter & chocolate chip cookies, and you'll have discovered your family's favorite. Enjoy!

Servings: 12

Preparation time: 25 minutes

Ingredients:

- 1/3 cup gluten-free oats
- ½ tsp. baking powder
- 2 large eggs
- ¼ tsp. salt
- 1 cup sugar
- ¼ cup vegetable oil
- 1 cup semisweet chocolate chips
- 1 tsp. vanilla extract
- 1 cup peanut butter

Directions:

Preheat the oven to 325°F.

Line a sheet pan with parchment paper.

Mix together the sugar, peanut butter, chocolate chips, oats, oil, baking powder, eggs, vanilla, and salt in a sizable bowl.

Drop the cookie dough onto the sizable sheet pan using a sizable tablespoon.

Bake the cookie dough for about 15 minutes, or until just golden brown.

Cool before serving.

Conclusion

Thank you for reading this book. I hope that you enjoyed it. Are you ready to start making some gluten-free recipes?

If you want to make some delicious meals with these recipes, go ahead and get the book. It will be the best investment that you have ever made. After your first time trying one of these recipes, you will never be able to go back. These recipes are healthy, delicious, and easy to prepare.

Author's Afterthoughts

Thanks ever so much to each of my cherished readers for investing the time to read this book!

I know you could have picked from many other books, but you chose this one. So, a big thanks for reading all the way to the end. If you enjoyed this book or received value from it, I'd like to ask you for a favor. Please take a few minutes to **post an honest and heartfelt review on Amazon.com.** Your support does make a difference and helps to benefit other people.

Thanks!

Julia Chiles

Printed in Poland
by Amazon Fulfillment
Poland Sp. z o.o., Wrocław
16 December 2021

abbfabf8-8dc1-4876-8d4a-809666d3e8c8R01